Pacific Coast Fern Finder

by Glenn Keator, Ph.D, and
Ruth M. Heady
illustrated by Valerie R. Winemiller

Reflection in Stone

Locked in stone, fern frond,
crushed by foot of mastodon,
mirrors spike and blade
of Botrychium growing
at my feet, sheltered by stone.

—Ruth

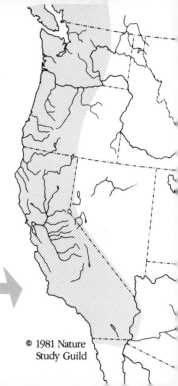

to use this book

1. Observe the features which will identify your fern. Note:

   - any non-green spore-producing structures,

   - whether there's more than one kind of frond,

   - whether the fern creeps or grows in clumps,

   - whether it grows on rocks, bark, or in soil.

2. Then turn to page 7, make the first choice and go on from there.

3. See pages 30 - 35 for a guide to some common ferns.

4. See the introductory pages for general information about ferns.

area covered by this book

This book identifies native Pacific coast ferns, clubmosses, spikemosses, quillworts and horsetails, excluding some rare or very restricted species. The relationship between these plant groups is outlined on page 6.

© 1981 Nature Study Guild

abbreviations for habitat, range and altitude

Information about each species illustrated in this book is printed in a green-letter code like this ➔

Sh Ro +Gr ← habitat information (top line)
Ca—Bc /Co ← range information (middle line)
3—9.5 ← altitude information (bottom line)

---

habitat code

Sh	shady forests
Ps	partly shaded forests, woods
Op	open, sunny areas
So	soil which roots can penetrate
Ro	rocky areas, crevices, ledges
Ep	mossy logs, bark (epiphytes)
St	streamsides, springs, by moving water
Ac	acid soils
Gr	granite, granitic soils
Ls	limestone, limestone soils
Bo	bogs, ponds, vernal pools, usually stagnant water

---

modifying symbols

The meanings of habitat and range codes may be altered by prefixes:

+	mostly, as in +Ls (mostly on limestone)
–	seldom, as in –Mt (seldom in mountains)
/	not, as in /De (not in desert)

---

range code

Ca	California
Or	Oregon
Wa	Washington
Bc	British Columbia
Mt	mountains
Ft	foothills
Co	coastal areas
De	deserts
Sn	Sierra Nevada
Pc	Pacific coast—whole area covered by this book

Compass prefixes or cn (central) may modify the range codes so that, for instance, cn—neCa would mean central to northeastern California.

---

altitude code

Altitude ranges are in thousands of feet, so that 5.5—10 indicates from 5,500 to 10,000 feet above sea level. ? means we don't know.

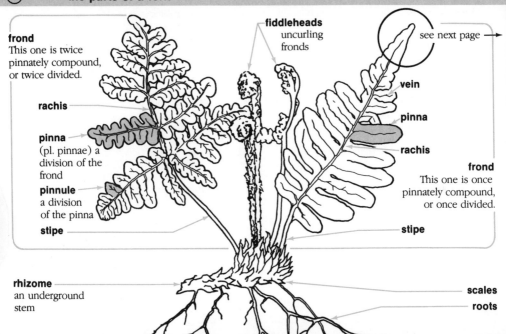

frond
This one is twice pinnately compound, or twice divided.

rachis

pinna
(pl. pinnae) a division of the frond

pinnule
a division of the pinna

stipe

fiddleheads
uncurling fronds

see next page →

vein

pinna

rachis

frond
This one is once pinnately compound, or once divided.

stipe

rhizome
an underground stem

scales

roots

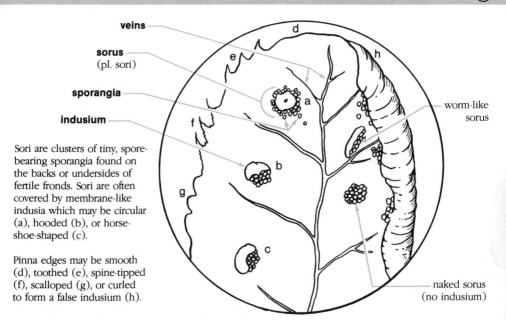

veins

sorus
(pl. sori)

sporangia

indusium

worm-like sorus

Sori are clusters of tiny, spore-bearing sporangia found on the backs or undersides of fertile fronds. Sori are often covered by membrane-like indusia which may be circular (a), hooded (b), or horse-shoe-shaped (c).

Pinna edges may be smooth (d), toothed (e), spine-tipped (f), scalloped (g), or curled to form a false indusium (h).

naked sorus (no indusium)

Like other plants, ferns can reproduce vegetatively by the breakup of their rhizomes. They also reproduce sexually, but unlike flowering plants they use spores rather than seeds, and generate new ferns from an alternate generation of plants which look nothing like ferns.

The familiar fern plant is called a sporophyte plant (1). When mature it forms sori (2), usually on the undersides of the fronds. Each sorus has many sporangia (3) where a kind of cell division called meiosis produces spores with only one set of chromosomes (haploid) instead of the two complete sets (diploid) present in each cell of the sporophyte.

When a sporangium is ripe, the thin lip cells (4) in its helmet-shaped annulus (5) burst from water pressure, snapping the sporangium backward and hurling the tiny spores (6) forward to ride the wind.

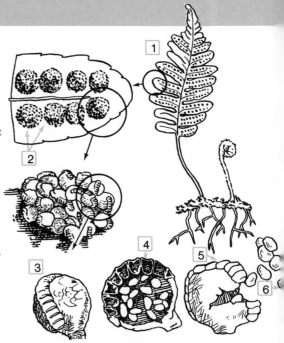

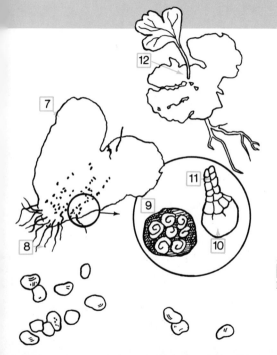

If they land where there is the right combination of moisture, light, temperature, and space, the spores grow into a prothallus or gametophyte plant (7). The best place to see prothalli is on moist, shaded banks. They are thin, flat, heart-shaped plants about a centimeter long, with hair-like rhizoids (8) instead of roots. They are often mistaken for liverworts. Prothalli grow tiny sexual reproductive containers on their bottom sides: globe-shaped antheridia (9) with coiled sperms inside; and archegonia (10), each with a single egg. The sperms swim about in a thin film of water and, if successful, go down the neck (11) of an archegonium to fertilize the egg and form a zygote (diploid). The zygote grows rapidly into an embryo fern plant which is at first nourished and protected by the prothallus to which it's still attached. But soon the young fern bursts through the prothallus (12), sinks a root and lifts a frond. The spent prothallus withers.

This book is about ferns and fern relatives, plants which never bear seeds. Of these plants, true ferns have large leaves with many veins. The rest have scales or small leaves with single veins. Of those with single veins, the following fern relatives are in this book:

- Equisetums have jointed stems, scale-like leaves, and produce spores in cones.
- Isoetes have grass-like leaves swollen at the base with spores inside, and live in wet places.
- Selaginellas have green, moss-like leaves and tiny green cones which produce spores.
- Lycopodiums have green, moss-like leaves and larger, usually non-green cones which produce spores.

Plants which aren't in this book include seed-bearing plants, both gymnosperms, which produce seeds in cones, and angiosperms (flowering plants) which produce their seeds inside ovaries which become fruits. Also not in this book are non-seed-bearing plants which have no leaves, or have leaf-like scales with no veins. Plants with leaf-like structures but no veins include these groups:

- Mosses form leafy cushions close to the ground, and produce spore-bearing capsules on slender stalks.
- Liverworts form branched, green ribbons next to the soil, with umbrella-like reproductive structures.

Algae, fungi and lichens usually lack leaf-like structures altogether, although the brown algae, which live in salt water, sometimes have them (as in kelps). Lichens, too, sometimes have leaf-like or ribbon-like forms, but differ from liverworts by producing cup-like reproductive structures.

Begin here.

If the plant's leaves are:

- small, moss-like, go to ⟶ p. 11
- like a four-leaf clover, go to **Marsilea**, p. 39.
- sheath-like on a jointed, green stem, go to **Equisetum**, p. 27.
- none of the above, go to ⟶ below

 If plants float on water, go to **Azolla**, p. 17.

If not, go to ⟶

 If leaves are tongue-shaped, go to **Ophioglossum**, p. 42.

If leaves are grass-like, and:

- thickened at the base, go to **Isoetes**, p. 36.
- not thickened, but curled in a fiddlehead when young, go to **Pilularia**, p. 48.

If leaves are neither grass-like nor tongue-shaped, go to next page

If each frond has both a fertile part and a sterile part; the spore bodies (sporangia) clustered like grape bunches, go to **Botrychium**, p. 18.

If each frond is either completely fertile or completely sterile, it is a true fern. Go to ———————————————→

If sterile and fertile fronds are shaped alike, and differ only by presence or absence of sori, go to ———————————————→

If sterile and fertile fronds differ by shape, go to

If fronds are gold or silver on the underside, go to **Pityrogramma**, p. 48.

If not, and sori are:

- near the pinna edge, go to 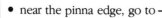 ———————————————→ next page
- away from the edge, go to ———————————————→ 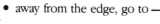 p. 10

If fronds are two or more times divided, go to **Cryptogramma**, p. 21.

If they're divided only once, go to **Blechnum**, p. 17.

If pinnae are fan- or crescent-shaped, delicate, go to **Adiantum**, p. 12.

If they're some other shape, firm or tough, go to

If frond outline is a long, narrow triangle like this

go to

If the outline is a broader triangle,
and frond width is:

- less than 15cm, go to **Aspidotis**, p. 14.
- more than 30cm, go to **Pteridium**, p. 49.

If pinnae curl to form an indusium, and:

- have hairs or scales, go to **Cheilanthes**, p. 22.
- lack hairs and scales, go to **Pellaea**, p. 43.

If pinnae do not curl to form an indusium, go to **Notholaena**, p. 40.

If sori have an indusium (look at young, green sori), go to

If not, and fronds are:
- bunched, rhizomes scaly, go to ——————————————→
- single, rhizomes not scaly, go to **Polypodium**, p. 46.

If fronds are once pinnately divided, go to

If they're twice or more pinnately divided, go to ——→  next page

If the pinnae have projections at their bases like this ——→

and indusia are umbrella-like, go to **Polystichum**, p. 50.

If pinnae lack projections; and indusia are horseshoe-shaped, go to **Dryopteris**, p. 24.

If fronds are three times pinnately divided, delicate, go to **Athyrium**, p. 16.

If they're once or twice divided, go to **Thelypteris**, p. 57.

If sori are worm-like, arranged in chains, go to **Woodwardia**, p. 59.

If sori are rounded, or not in chains; and fronds are:

- over 30cm long, go to ⟶
- shorter, go to ⟶

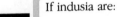

If indusia are:

- umbrella-shaped (fronds stiff), go to **Polystichum**, p. 50.
- horseshoe-shaped (fronds stiff), go to **Dryopteris**, p. 24.
- crescent-shaped (fronds delicate), go to **Athyrium**, p. 16.

If sori are oblong to linear, go to **Asplenium**, p. 15.

If they're rounded, and:

- indusia form hoods (look at young sori), go to **Cystopteris**, p. 24.
- indusia split into star-like strips and are partly covered by the spore bodies, go to **Woodsia**, p. 58.

If plant bears obvious cones (and cone scales are usually whitish), go to **Lycopodium**, p. 36.

If cones are inconspicuous, with green scales, go to **Selaginella**, p. 54.

(12) ## *Adiantum*

These are delicate, moisture-loving ferns with dark, shiny, nearly black stipes. Their fragile pinnae have a distinctive, dichotomous vein pattern. The pinna edges curl to form false indusia over the sori. Adiantums grow on rocky slopes where their roots can penetrate moist crevices. California Indians wove the black stipes into designs on their baskets.

If whole frond is forked at its base and is as wide as long, it is **Five-Finger Fern**
Adiantum pedatum

Winter-dormant.

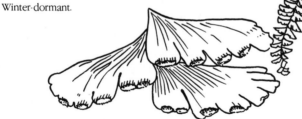

If frond is narrower, unforked at base, go to

 next page

Sh Ro St
Pc /De
0—10

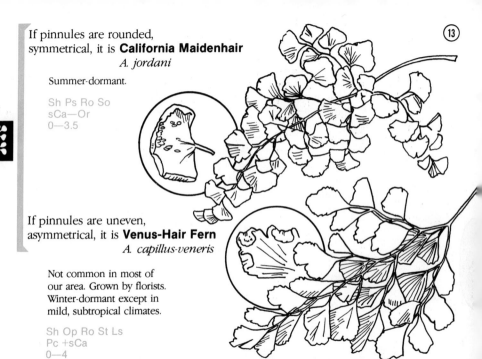

If pinnules are rounded,
symmetrical, it is **California Maidenhair**
A. jordani

Summer-dormant.

Sh Ps Ro So
sCa—Or
0—3.5

If pinnules are uneven,
asymmetrical, it is **Venus-Hair Fern**
A. capillus-veneris

Not common in most of
our area. Grown by florists.
Winter-dormant except in
mild, subtropical climates.

Sh Op Ro St Ls
Pc +sCa
0—4

Aspidotis

These small rock ferns have shiny, dark stipes, fronds of broad outline, and false indusia formed by curled-under pinnule edges. The two species have distinctive pinnule and sorus patterns, but hybrids between them, referred to as *A. carlotta-hallii,* show intermediate features and occur where species' ranges overlap as in Marin County, California. These ferns have been referred to other closely related genera; some authors place them in *Cheilanthes* or *Pellaea.*

Op Ro Gr
cnCa—sBc
1—8.5

If smallest frond segments are narrow, undivided, it is **Oregon Cliffbrake Indian's Dream**
Aspidotis densa

Sori are continuous. Different ecological races may exist on serpentine, granite, etc.

If frond segments are deeply redivided or lobed, it is **California Lace Fern**
A. californica

Sori are small, separate.

Sh Ro
Ca /De
0—2.5

Asplenium

These small rock ferns are uncommon, particularly in California. The genus is large and contains many tropical epiphytic ferns such as the familiar house plant, bird's nest fern (*A. nidus*). The long sori located away from the pinnule edge identify the genus. Sori are protected by long, narrow indusia attached along one side.

If pinnae are shallowly scalloped,
it is **Maidenhair Spleenwort**
    Asplenium trichomanes

    Rachis is hairless.

If they're deeply scalloped, and
end of rachis is:

- stiff, shiny, purple-brown,
  it is **Western Spleenwort**
      A. vespertinum

- soft, green,
  it is **Green Spleenwort**
      A. viride

Sh Ro Ls
+Bc—Wa –Or—Ca
?

Sh Ro St
sCa Mt
0—3

Op Ps Ro St Ls
Or—Bc
0—4

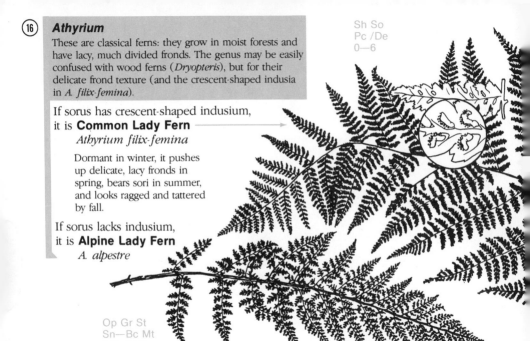

(16) **Athyrium**

These are classical ferns: they grow in moist forests and have lacy, much divided fronds. The genus may be easily confused with wood ferns (*Dryopteris*), but for their delicate frond texture (and the crescent-shaped indusia in *A. filix-femina*).

If sorus has crescent-shaped indusium,
it is **Common Lady Fern** ——————→
    Athyrium filix-femina

> Dormant in winter, it pushes up delicate, lacy fronds in spring, bears sori in summer, and looks ragged and tattered by fall.

If sorus lacks indusium,
it is **Alpine Lady Fern**
    A. alpestre

Sh So
Pc /De
0—6

Op Gr St
Sn—Bc Mt
5.5—11.5

Azolla

The one Pacific coast species, duck fern, is highly specialized to float on water. Each plant consists of a tiny body with snowflake-like fronds (often tinted red when growing in full sun) and root-like hairs extending 2 to 5mm into the water. Reproduction is mostly by fragmentation. Sexual reproduction is complex, with two kinds of spores and prothalli as in the pepperworts. Duck fern quickly covers sluggish ponds and bodies of stagnant water, often competing with the tiny, bright green, floating duckweed (*Lemna* spp.), a flowering plant. The apt common name, duck fern, alludes to plants travelling from pond to pond on ducks' feet.

Blechnum

The species found here, deer fern, is widely distributed through northern regions of the world. It grows in moist forests, and is one of the few ferns to survive the extremely acidic conditions of sphagnum bogs. Deer fern fronds taper toward both tip and base. Sword fern fronds are similar, but wider at the base. In summer, deer fern bears distinctive central plumes of erect, fertile fronds with narrow pinnae entirely covered by sori underneath.

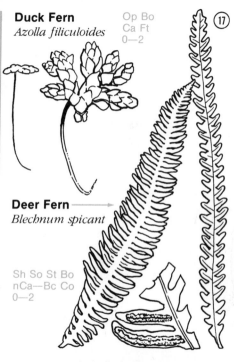

Duck Fern
Azolla filiculoides

Op Bo
Ca Ft
0—2

(17)

Deer Fern
Blechnum spicant

Sh So St Bo
nCa—Bc Co
0—2

Botrychium

You're lucky to find one of these uncommon ferns. *Botrychium* and *Ophioglossum* are the two primitive fern genera which form no fiddleheads on young fronds. Each growing season they make a single pinnately compound frond with two different parts: one sterile, the other fertile with hundreds of grape-like sporangia rather than true sori. The two frond parts may look like two separate fronds if junction between them is underground. The species vary considerably, and minor varieties are not distinguished here.

If frond segments
are rounded, go to ● p. 20

If they're blunt
or pointed, go to ★ next page

Op St Gr
cnCa—Bc
0—8

If sterile and fertile blades seem separate
because they are joined underground,
it is **Leatherleaf Grape Fern** (illus. p. 18)
    Botrychium multifidum

If they're joined above ground; and plant is:

- over 30cm tall; frond at least twice divided,
  it is **Virginia Grape Fern**
      B. virginianum ⟶

- under 30cm tall; frond once divided,
  it is **Lanceleaf Grape Fern**
      B. lanceolatum

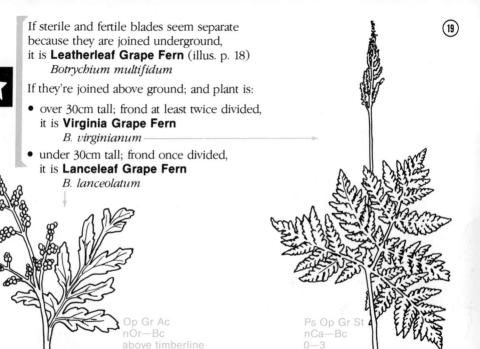

Op Gr Ac
nOr—Bc
above timberline

Ps Op Gr St
nCa—Bc
0—3

If frond is divided only once, and has fan-shaped or halfmoon-shaped segments, it is **Moonwort** ————————→

Botrychium lunaria

If frond is divided more than once and has segments of another shape, it is **Simple Grape Fern**

B. simplex

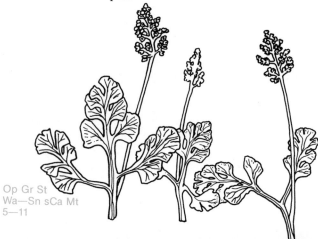

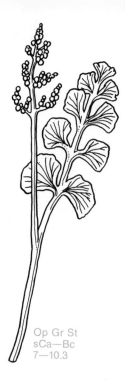

Cryptogramma

These small rock ferns grow in mountains and are dormant under winter snow. Their coarse frond segments look like parsley, especially on first-developed sterile fronds. In summer, there are central fronds with narrow, sorus-producing segments. Look for these bright green ferns next to paler or grayer pellaea among granite rocks.

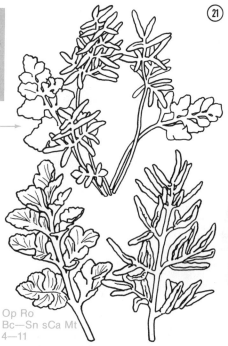

If fronds are clumped; pinnae firm and tough, it is **Common Parsley Fern** ────────→
  Cryptogramma acrostichoides

If fronds are arrayed along a creeping rhizome; pinnae thin and delicate, it is **Slender Parsley Fern**
  C. stelleri

Sh Ro Ls
Bc—neOr
?

Op Ro
Bc—Sn sCa Mt
4—11

Cheilanthes

These specialized rock ferns grow on hot slopes devoid of surface moisture except in winter or early spring. Roots reach deep into rock crevices for moisture. Fronds curl up during hottest months, uncurling after rains. Fronds are further protected by scales and/or hairs which reflect light and heat. Most cheilanthes have a false indusium (which distinguishes them from notholaenas) formed by the curling of the pinnule edge. Pinnules are rounded or bead-like.

If pinnules curl to form a continuous indusium, go to

Op Ro Ls
sOr—cnCa Sn
0—2

If not, it is **Cooper's Lip Fern**
Cheilanthes cooperae

 If fronds are divided three or more times and not heavily wooly underneath, go to

next page

If they're only twice divided, and heavily wooly underneath, it is **Lace Fern**
C. gracillima

Op Ro
Bc—nCa Sn
2.5—9

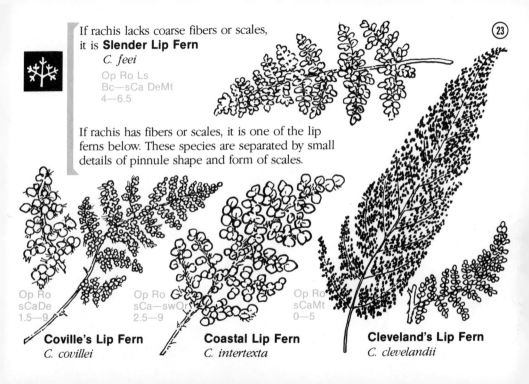

If rachis lacks coarse fibers or scales,
it is **Slender Lip Fern**
C. feei
Op Ro Ls
Bc—sCa DeMt
4—6.5

If rachis has fibers or scales, it is one of the lip
ferns below. These species are separated by small
details of pinnule shape and form of scales.

Op Ro
sCaDe
1.5—9

Coville's Lip Fern
C. covillei

Op Ro
sCa—swOr
2.5—9

Coastal Lip Fern
C. intertexta

Op Ro
sCaMt
0—5

Cleveland's Lip Fern
C. clevelandii

Cystopteris

The species found here, bladder fern, is a small woodland and mountain rock fern that grows on partly shaded, moist, rocky banks, often by streams or seeps. Its fronds resemble those of young lady ferns, but its sori are rounded and have a hood-shaped indusium arched over the sorus at one end. Observe this on young, green sori before the indusium shrivels as the sorus turns brown.

Bladder Fern
Fragile Fern
Cystopteris fragilis

Sh Ro So
Pc /De
0—12

Dryopteris

This is a confusing, variable genus of medium-sized forest ferns—some have once divided fronds, others with fronds divided several times resemble lady fern or bracken. But sorus shapes and indusium details differ. Dryopterises usually have rounded sori with horseshoe-shaped indusia, and their fronds feel tougher and firmer than the delicate lady fern. With practice, one can detect differences in frond patterns as well. Dryopterises are excellent garden plants. Once established, they require little care and remain green all year in mild climates.

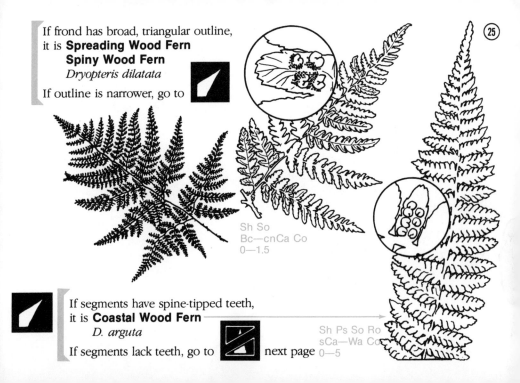

If frond has broad, triangular outline,
it is **Spreading Wood Fern**
Spiny Wood Fern
Dryopteris dilatata

If outline is narrower, go to 

Sh So
Bc—cnCa Co
0—1.5

If segments have spine-tipped teeth,
it is **Coastal Wood Fern**
D. arguta

If segments lack teeth, go to  next page

Sh Ps So Ro
sCa—Wa Co
0—5

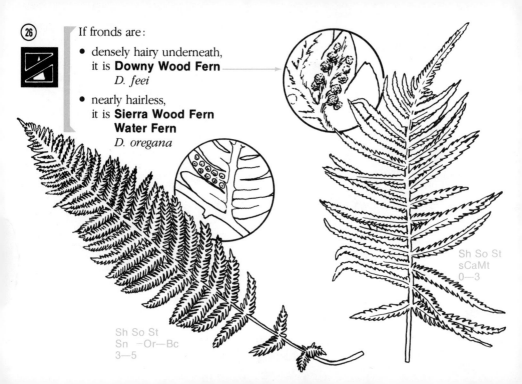

(26)

If fronds are:

- densely hairy underneath,
  it is **Downy Wood Fern**
  D. feei

- nearly hairless,
  it is **Sierra Wood Fern**
  Water Fern
  D. oregana

Sh So St
sCaMt
0—3

Sh So St
Sn –Or—Bc
3—5

Equisetum

Equisetums are living remnants of an ancient group which had giant tree-like forms. They have underground creeping rhizomes; green, hollow, jointed, ribbed stems impregnated with hard, glass-like silica; brownish to grey leaves which form a sheath around each node; spores produced inside tight, brown to black, warty cones. Some species bear cones on non-green stalks which arise in early spring before the green vegetative shoots; others bear cones at the ends of ordinary green shoots. Unbranched species are called scouring rush because their silica can scour pots and pans like fine sandpaper. Branched ones look feathery and are called horsetail. Peeled stems are edible but tedious to prepare. Equisetums absorb unusual soil minerals like gold. They may invade gardens, and can push up asphalt as they spread.

If main stems bear whorled side branches like this (cone tips are rounded), go to ⟶

If whorled side branches are missing (cone tips are sharply pointed), go to ⟶ p. 29

If plants grow in standing water or directly next to permanent streams, go to ⟶

If they grow elsewhere, it is **Common Horsetail**
Equisetum arvense

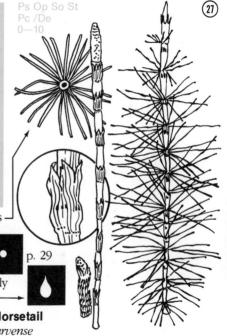

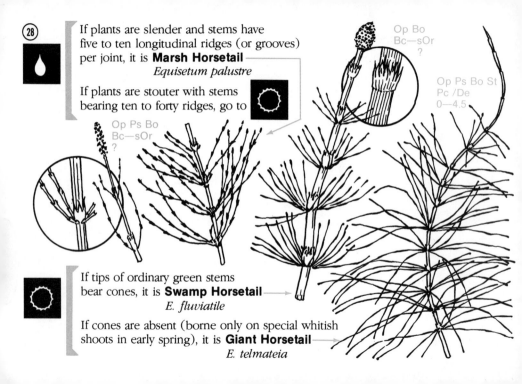

(28)

If plants are slender and stems have five to ten longitudinal ridges (or grooves) per joint, it is **Marsh Horsetail** *Equisetum palustre*

Op Bo
Bc—sOr
?

If plants are stouter with stems bearing ten to forty ridges, go to

Op Ps Bo St
Pc /De
0—4.5

Op Ps Bo
Bc—sOr
?

If tips of ordinary green stems bear cones, it is **Swamp Horsetail** *E. fluviatile*

If cones are absent (borne only on special whitish shoots in early spring), it is **Giant Horsetail** *E. telmateia*

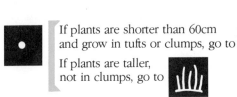

 If plants are shorter than 60cm and grow in tufts or clumps, go to

If plants are taller, not in clumps, go to

 If main stem is hollow, it is **Northern Scouring Rush** —
E. variegatum

If it's solid, it is **Dwarf Scouring Rush** —
E. scirpoides

 If stems feel smooth, and each leaf sheath has only one dark black band, it is **Smooth Scouring Rush** —
E. laevigatum

If stems are rough and each sheath has a double dark band (one at base and one at top), it is **Common Scouring Rush** —
E. hymale

Sh Op St
Bc—Wa
?

Ps Op St
Bc—Or Mt
?

Op Ps St
Pc /De
0—6.5

Ps Op St
Pc /De
0—8.5

29

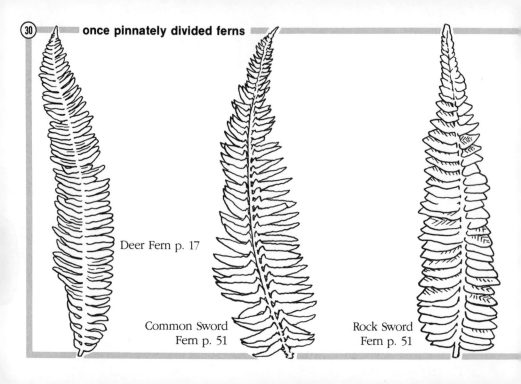

Deer Fern p. 17

Common Sword
Fern p. 51

Rock Sword
Fern p. 51

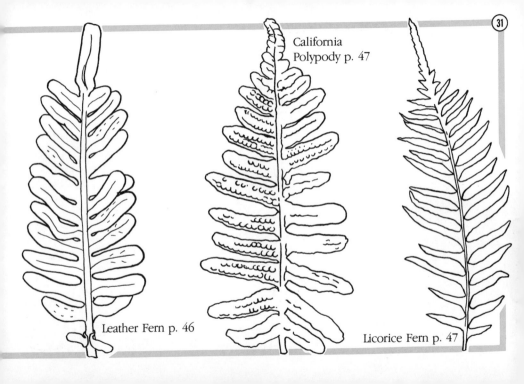

California
Polypody p. 47

Leather Fern p. 46

Licorice Fern p. 47

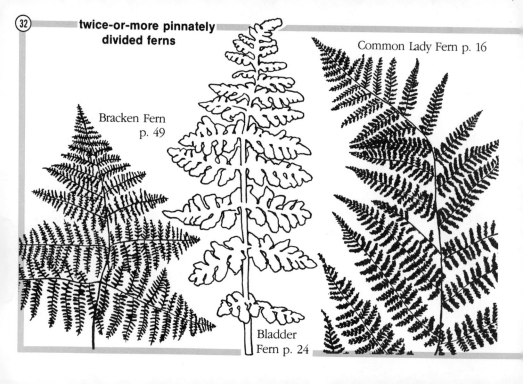

Common Lady Fern p. 16

Bracken Fern p. 49

Bladder Fern p. 24

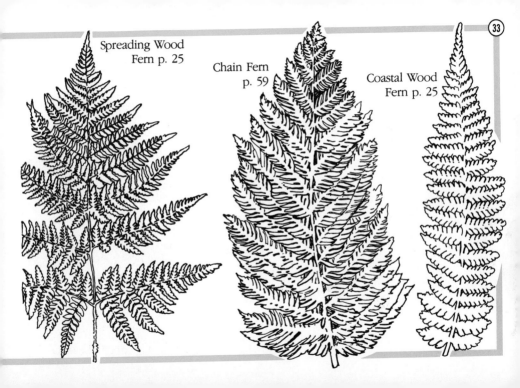

Spreading Wood
Fern p. 25

Chain Fern
p. 59

Coastal Wood
Fern p. 25

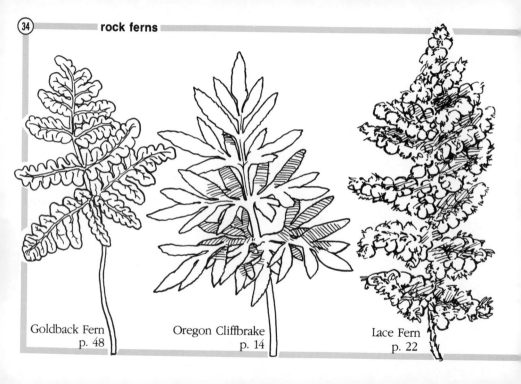

Goldback Fern
p. 48

Oregon Cliffbrake
p. 14

Lace Fern
p. 22

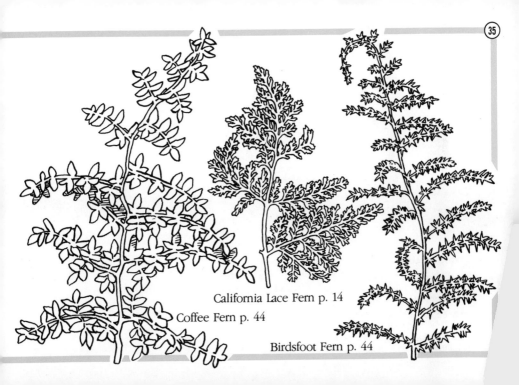

California Lace Fern p. 14

Coffee Fern p. 44

Birdsfoot Fern p. 44

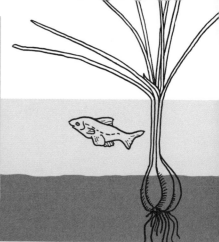

Isoetes

Identification of the several species is based mostly on microscopic details of megaspores not enumerated here. The species fall into two habitat groups: those totally submerged and those growing on the margins of water with leaves clearly above the surface. Isoetes are seldom noticed because their leaves resemble tufts of grass. But the translucency of their leaves, their aquatic habitat, and their enlarged, white leaf bases (just below the soil surface) distinguish them from other grass-like plants. The enlarged leaf bases contain the spore bodies and are attached to nugget-like, food-storing corms. Some quillworts live in vernal pools and go dormant during summer and early fall.

Lycopodium

Lycopodium leaves are moss-like, but have a true midvein. They differ from selaginellas in their cones, which are usually conspicuous and produce only one kind of spore; and in their leaves, which tend to be longer and coarser. This ancient genus is largely tropical, but isolated colonies occur n California, and several species live in the rain forests of Oregon, Washington and British Columbia. Lycopodiums have been used for antiseptics (spores sprinkled on wounds) or as explosives (dried spores). The leafy branches are gathered for Christmas decoration as replacement for fir boughs.

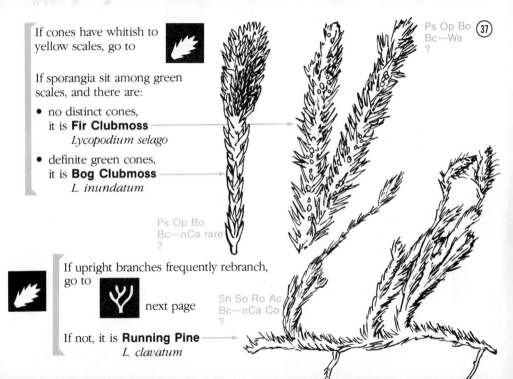

If cones have whitish to yellow scales, go to Ps Op Bo Bc—Wa ? 37

If sporangia sit among green scales, and there are:

- no distinct cones, it is **Fir Clubmoss**
  Lycopodium selago

- definite green cones, it is **Bog Clubmoss**
  L. inundatum

Ps Op Bo Bc—nCa rare ?

If upright branches frequently rebranch, go to

next page

Sh So Ro Ac Bc—nCa Co ?

If not, it is **Running Pine**
L. clavatum

If cones are separated from green leaves by a nearly leafless stalk, go to

If cones sit directly above green leaves, it is **Ground Pine**
L. obscurum

Op Sh Bo Ac
Bc—nOr
?

Sh So Ro Ac
Bc—Wa
?

If leaves are stiff and symmetrical, sometimes flattened, it is **Ground Cedar**
L. complanatum

If they're spirally arranged, never flattened, it is **Alaska Clubmoss**
L. sitchense

Sh Op Gr
Bc—nOr Mt
?

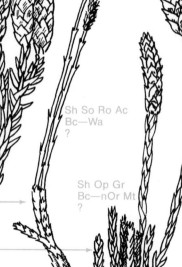

Marsilea

These are specialized water ferns with roots and rhizomes in mud. The stipes rise through the water and the four pinnae float on the surface. Fiddleheads form below the surface. Fertile fronds are highly modified, bean-shaped structures close to the submerged rhizome which produce two kinds of sporangia: some make large megaspores which develop into female prothalli bearing archegonia and eggs; others produce tiny microspores which develop into male prothalli with antheridia and sperms. Few ferns have a life cycle of such complexity. One species occurs here.

Pepperwort
Clover Fern
Marsilea vestita

Op Bo
Pc /De
0—7

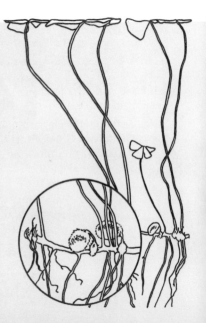

Notholaena

These rock ferns are well adapted to desert mountains. Their fronds conserve moisture with cottony hairs and/or glandular secretions. In drought, they also curl up and become dormant. They are allied to the lip ferns or cheilanthes, but lack their indusium-like curled pinnule edges.

If frond outline is long and narrow, go to

If it's a broad triangle, it is **California Cloak Fern**
Notholaena californica

Op Ro
sCa DeMt
0—2.5

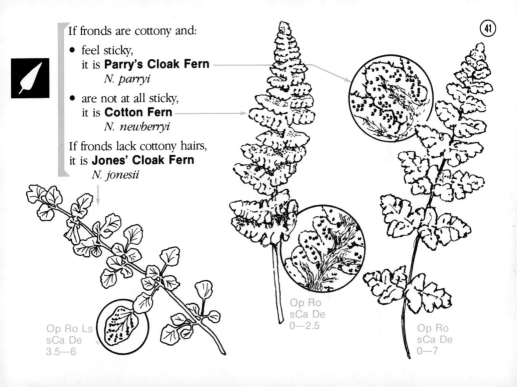

If fronds are cottony and:

- feel sticky,
  it is **Parry's Cloak Fern**
    N. parryi

- are not at all sticky,
  it is **Cotton Fern**
    N. newberryi

If fronds lack cottony hairs,
it is **Jones' Cloak Fern**
    N. jonesii

41

Op Ro Ls
sCa De
3.5—6

Op Ro
sCa De
0—2.5

Op Ro
sCa De
0—7

Ophioglossum

These ferns are even rarer than the grape ferns, small, and easily overlooked. They are abundant in the tropics where they grow as epiphytes on trees. Like *Botrychium*, the genus is primitive: does not form fiddleheads, lacks true sori, and makes only one frond per growing season. The two-parted frond has a long, green sterile tongue joined to a smaller green tongue with rows of grape-like sporangia, hence the name adder's tongue.

If sterile part of frond is broad, elliptical to ovate, with more than eight longitudinal veins, it is **Common Adder's Tongue**
Ophioglossum vulgatum

If sterile part is narrower, mostly lance-shaped, with fewer longitudinal veins, it is **California Adder's Tongue**
O. californicum

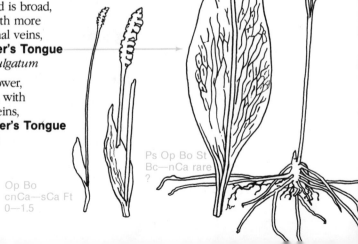

Ps Op Bo St
Bc—nCa rare
?

Op Bo
cnCa—sCa Ft
0—1.5

Pellaea

Pellaeas grow most often on hot, exposed rocks or on rocky slopes in open woods, and are not so typical of deserts as are cheilanthes and notholaenas. They often grow with goldback fern, Oregon cliffbrake, or sometimes with the bead ferns. They are distinguished by the lack of wooly or cottony hairs, and the complete absence of gold or silver powder on the frond backs. Most often the pinnules are dusty grey or blue-green, and their edges curl to form false indusia for the sori.

If fronds are divided only once, go to

If they're divided two or more times, go to next page

If pinnae are partly divided, mitten-shaped, it is **Brewer's Cliffbrake** — *Pellaea breweri*

If they're undivided and tough, it is **Bridges' Cliffbrake** — *P. bridgesii*

If pinnae are rounded at
the tips, not pointed,
it is **Coffee Fern**
P. andromedaefolia

> Name refers to brown of
> fronds in late summer.

If tips are sharply pointed
(look carefully),
go to

If fronds are divided three
times toward the base,
it is **Birdsfoot Fern**
P. mucronata

> A tea has been brewed from
> the fronds of this species.

If they're divided only twice
throughout, go to **2** next page

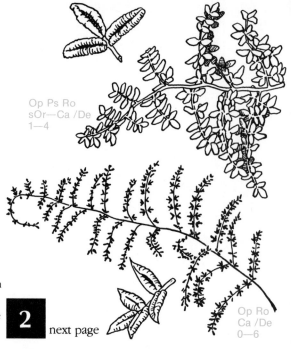

Op Ps Ro
sOr—Ca /De
1—4

Op Ro
Ca /De
0—6

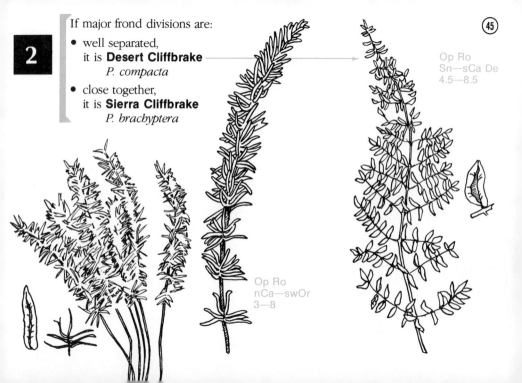

If major frond divisions are:

- well separated,
  it is **Desert Cliffbrake** →
  P. compacta

- close together,
  it is **Sierra Cliffbrake**
  P. brachyptera

2

(45)

Op Ro
Sn—sCa De
4.5—8.5

Op Ro
nCa—swOr
3—8

(46) ## *Polypodium*

These small ferns seldom grow directly in soil. They are epiphytic on tree bark in moist coastal forests, or grow on mossy rock shelves and cliffs in woodlands or along sea bluffs. The creeping rhizomes are usually hidden among mosses. The fronds are once pinnately divided and bear nearly circular sori which lack indusia.

If fronds are firm, leathery,
with sori 3mm or more across,
it is **Leather Fern**
Polypodium scouleri

If fronds are thin, with smaller
sori, go to ⟶

Ps Sh Ep
cnCa—Bc Co
0—1.5

  If fronds are longer than 15cm;
and segments have toothed edges,
go to

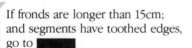 next page

If fronds are shorter; segments
rounded with smooth or scalloped edges,
it is **Western Polypody**
P. hesperium

Ro Ep Op
Pc rare
5—8.5

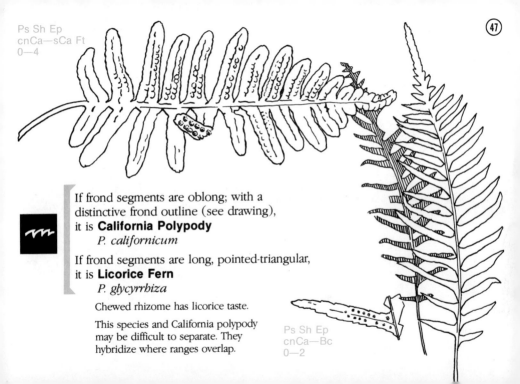

If frond segments are oblong; with a
distinctive frond outline (see drawing),
it is **California Polypody**
 P. californicum

If frond segments are long, pointed-triangular,
it is **Licorice Fern**
 P. glycyrrhiza

Chewed rhizome has licorice taste.

This species and California polypody
may be difficult to separate. They
hybridize where ranges overlap.

Pilularia

These are called pillworts. They're closely related to the
pepperworts, and resemble them in most respects, but
pillworts lack broad pinnae. Technically, the uncurled
grass-like leaf is just a modified stipe or frond stalk.
Pillworts live mostly in vernal pools and are dormant
in the dry season. One species is found here.

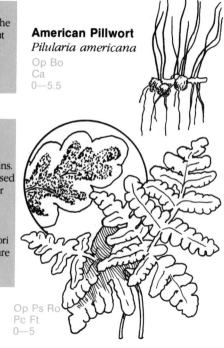

American Pillwort
Pilularia americana
Op Bo
Ca
0—5.5

Pityrogramma

The one species found here is a common rock fern
whose habitats range from moist, shaded rocks in
redwood forest openings to hot, rocky desert mountains.
The species has been divided into several varieties based
on frond size, coarseness of frond segments, and color
of the waxy powder on the frond back (either gold
or silver). All varieties have shiny, dark stipes, broad,
triangular fronds which curl up when dry, and a waxy
powder which you can rub off to make a print. The sori
form a brown network along the veins and may obscure
the powder on older fronds. This fern grows with
polypodies, pellaeas, and sometimes with cheilanthes.

Goldback Fern
Silverback Fern
Pityrogramma triangularis

Op Ps Ro
Pc Ft
0—5

Pteridium

The one species in this genus, bracken, is the most widespread and variable fern recognized. It ranges from the subarctic to the tropics with numerous geographic and ecological races. Some botanists recognize several varieties or even species of bracken. In California it grows from sea-level sand dunes to high Sierra meadows, and is most common in grasslands and open forests. Fronds range from 30 to 100cm high depending on moisture and soil. This vigorous, invasive fern spreads by deeply seated rhizomes. Once established, it's hard to eradicate. It's distinguished from other lacy ferns by growing in large colonies, by fronds that die back in winter, by the broad, triangular outline of the frond, and by the tendency of pinna edges to curl even before the sori form. Sori form a continuous band which follows the pinna outline. Indians dug the rhizomes for their fibers and beat out a starchy material for emergency food. Fiddleheads are a food delicacy in several parts of the world, but large quantities are toxic, especially uncooked.

Bracken Fern
Pteridium aquilinum

Op Ps So
Pc /De
0—10

Polystichum

This variable genus contains some common, medium-to-large forest and rock ferns. Sori which are partly covered by umbrella-like indusia, and bases of pinnae which resemble sword hilts (hence the name, sword fern) differentiate this genus from others such as *Dryopteris*. Polystichums are evergreen, easily maintained in a shady garden, and drought tolerant when established. Indians cooked and ate the young fiddleheads.

If fronds are once pinnately divided throughout, go to

If they're divided two to three times, at least toward the base, go to ⟶ p. 52

If segments are holly-like, with teeth pointing outwards, it is **Holly Fern**
Polystichum lonchitis

This species encircles the globe in subarctic regions.

If segments are narrower, with teeth pointing toward the tips, go to next page

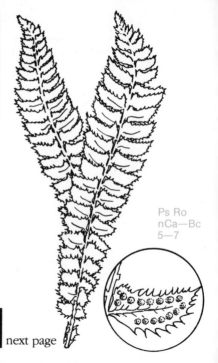

Ps Ro
nCa—Bc
5—7

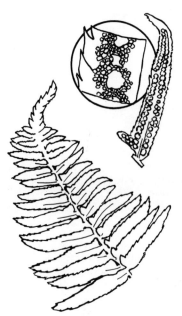

If rachis has scales (frond segments
are usually separate from one another),
it is **Common Sword Fern**
> *P. munitum*

> Covers whole hillsides
> with meter-long fronds
> in shady redwood forests.

If rachis is nearly naked
(frond segments closely overlap),
it is **Rock Sword Fern**
> *P. imbricans*

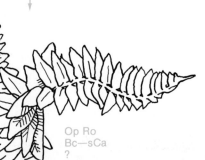

Op Ro
Bc—sCa
?

Ps Sh So
cnCa—Bc
0—2.5

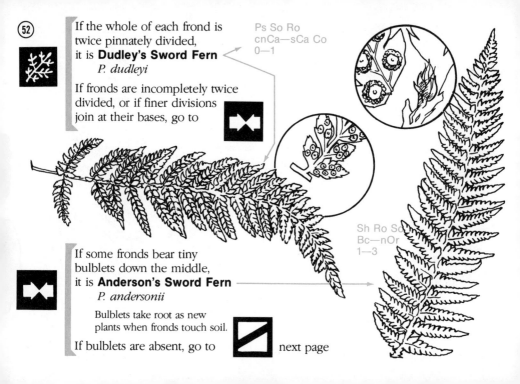

(52)

If the whole of each frond is twice pinnately divided, it is **Dudley's Sword Fern**
P. dudleyi

Ps So Ro
cnCa—sCa Co
0—1

If fronds are incompletely twice divided, or if finer divisions join at their bases, go to

If some fronds bear tiny bulblets down the middle, it is **Anderson's Sword Fern**
P. andersonii

Bulblets take root as new plants when fronds touch soil.

Sh Ro Sc
Bc—nOr
1—3

If bulblets are absent, go to next page

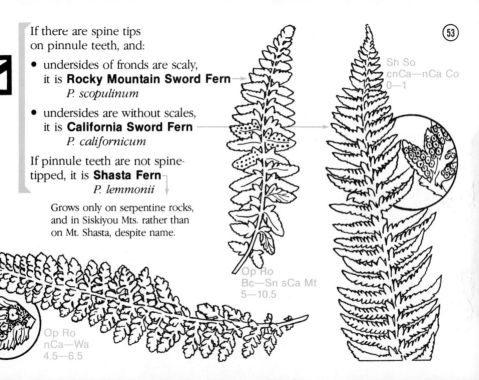

If there are spine tips
on pinnule teeth, and:

- undersides of fronds are scaly,
  it is **Rocky Mountain Sword Fern**
  P. scopulinum

- undersides are without scales,
  it is **California Sword Fern**
  P. californicum

If pinnule teeth are not spine-
tipped, it is **Shasta Fern**
P. lemmonii

Grows only on serpentine rocks,
and in Siskiyou Mts. rather than
on Mt. Shasta, despite name.

Sh So
cnCa—nCa Co
0—1

Op Ro
Bc—Sn sCa Mt
5—10.5

Op Ro
nCa—Wa
4.5—6.5

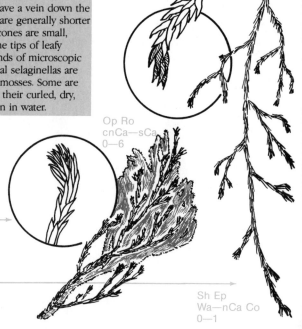

(54) *Selaginella*

Selaginellas are moss-like, but they have a vein down the center of each tiny leaf. Their leaves are generally shorter than those of lycopodiums, and the cones are small, green, difficult to discern, borne at the tips of leafy branches. The cones produce two kinds of microscopic spores. Some of the numerous tropical selaginellas are grown in terrariums and ferneries as mosses. Some are sold as "resurrection plants" because their curled, dry, brown branches unroll and turn green in water.

If leafy stems creep and root along the ground, go to

next page

If stems are upright and bushy, it is **Bushy Spikemoss** ————
Selaginella bigelovii

If stems hang or trail from tree branches; leaves wrinkled, it is **Festoon Spikemoss** ————
S. oregana

Op Ro
cnCa—sCa
0—6

Sh Ep
Wa—nCa Co
0—1

If leaves are of uniform size on all sides of stem,
go to next page

If they differ in size on the lower side of the stem,
go to

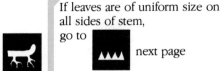

If leaves lie flat in definite rows, it is **Douglas' Spikemoss**
S. douglasii

If not, and leaves:

- turn purple with age, it is **Hansen's Spikemoss**
  S. hanseni

- remain green, it is **Rocky Mountain Spikemoss**
  S. scopulorum

Sh Ro
nCa—Wa
0—1

Op Ro
CaFt Sn
1—5

Op Ro
nCa—Bc
5—7

If leaf tips bear a yellowish bristle (use hand lens), it is **Watson's Spikemoss Alpine Spikemoss**
S. watsoni

If they bear a whitish bristle, and leaves are:

- greenish with short bristle tip, it is **Wallace's Spikemoss**
  S. wallacei

- blue-green with a longer bristle tip, it is **Blue Spikemoss**
  S. asprella

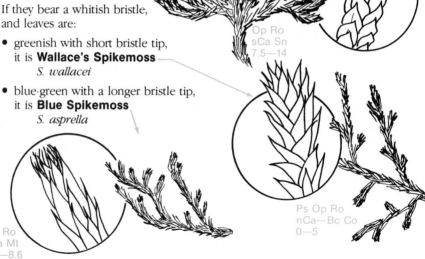

Op Ro
sCa Sn
7.5—14

Ps Op Ro
nCa—Bc Co
0—5

Op Ro
sCa Mt
5.5—8.6

Thelypteris

This genus is in dispute among botanists. Some place it in the variable genus, *Dryopteris*. We keep them separate here, however, because dryopterises have definite indusia which thelypterises lack. Thelypterises occur only in the northern portion of our range. They are much more typical of hardwood forests of the eastern U.S.

If frond is once pinnately divided,
with segments not notched,
it is **Beech Fern**
  Thelypteris phegopteris

If frond is twice pinnately divided,
with notched segments,
it is **Oak Fern**
  T. dryopteris

Ps So Ro
Bc—sOr
?

Sh So Ro
Bc—sOr
?

Woodsia

These small woodland and forest ferns have lacy fronds. They are uncommon and are something to search for. Their distinctive star-like indusia, which sit partly under the sporangia of the sori, separate them from the similar-looking bladder fern (*Cystopteris*).

Enlarged view of sorus

If fronds are hairy or sticky,
it is **Rocky Mountain Woodsia** ⟶
    Woodsia scopulina

If they're hairless and smooth,
it is **Oregon Woodsia** ↘
    W. oregana

Op Ro
Bc Sn sCa rare
4—11

Op Ro
Bc—Sn sCa Mt
4—12

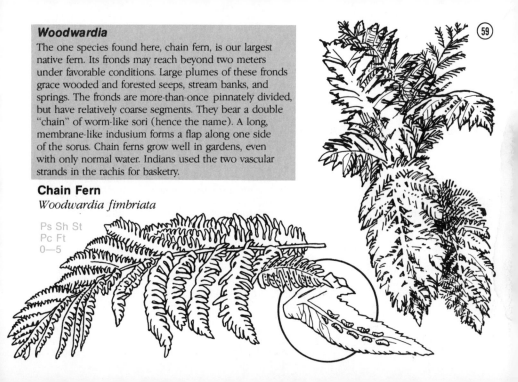

Woodwardia

The one species found here, chain fern, is our largest
native fern. Its fronds may reach beyond two meters
under favorable conditions. Large plumes of these fronds
grace wooded and forested seeps, stream banks, and
springs. The fronds are more-than-once pinnately divided,
but have relatively coarse segments. They bear a double
"chain" of worm-like sori (hence the name). A long,
membrane-like indusium forms a flap along one side
of the sorus. Chain ferns grow well in gardens, even
with only normal water. Indians used the two vascular
strands in the rachis for basketry.

Chain Fern
Woodwardia fimbriata

Ps Sh St
Pc Ft
0—5

Adder's-Tongue 42
Adian'tum capillus-ven'eris 13
A. jor'dani 13
A. peda'tum 12
Aspido'tis califor'nica 14
A. den'sa 14
Asple'nium tricho'manes 15
A. vesperti'num 15
A. vi'ride 15
Athy'rium alpes'tre 16
A. filix-fe'mina 16
Azo'lla filiculoi'des 17
Beech Fern 57
Birdsfoot Fern 44
Bladder Fern 24
Blech'num spi'cant 17
Botry'chium lanceola'tum 19
B. luna'ria 20
B. multi'fidum 19
B. sim'plex 20
B. virginia'num 19
Bracken Fern 49
Chain Fern 59
Cheilan'thes cleve'landii 23
C. coop'erae 22
C. covil'lei 23
C. fee'i 23
C. gracil'lima 22
C. intertex'ta 23

Cliffbrake, Brewer's 43
Cliffbrake, Bridges' 43
Cliffbrake, Desert 45
Cliffbrake, Oregon 14
Cliffbrake, Sierra 45
Cloak Fern, California 40
Cloak Fern, Jones' 41
Cloak Fern, Parry's 41
Clover Fern 39
Clubmoss, Alaska 38
Clubmoss, Bog 37
Clubmoss, Fir 37
Coffee Fern 44
Cotton Fern 41
Cryptogram'ma acrostichoi'des 21
C. stel'leri 21
Cystop'teris fra'gilis 24
Deer Fern 17
Dryop'teris argu'ta 25
D. dilata'ta 25
D. fee'i 26
D. orega'na 26
Duck Fern 17
Equise'tum arven'se 27
E. fluvia'tile 28
E. hyma'le 29
E. laeviga'tum 29
E. palus'tre 28
E. scirpoi'des 29

E. telmate'ia 28
E. variega'tum 29
Five-Finger Fern 12
Fragile Fern 24
Goldback Fern 48
Grape Fern, Lanceleaf 19
Grape Fern, Leatherleaf 19
Grape Fern, Simple 20
Grape Fern, Virginia 19
Ground Cedar 38
Ground Pine 38
Holly Fern 50
Horsetail, Common 27
Horsetail, Giant 28
Horsetail, Marsh 28
Horsetail, Swamp 28
Indian's Dream 14
Iso'etes 36
Lace Fern 22
Lace Fern, California 14
Lady Fern, Alpine 16
Lady Fern, Common 16
Leather Fern 46
Licorice Fern 47
Lip Fern, Cleveland's 23
Lip Fern, Coastal 23
Lip Fern, Cooper's 22
Lip Fern, Coville's 23
Lip Fern, Slender 23

Lycopo'dium clava'tum 37
L. complana'tum 38
L. inunda'tum 37
L. obscu'rum 38
L. sela'go 37
L. sitchen'se 38
Maidenhair, California 13
Marsi'lea vesti'ta 39
Moonwort 20
Notholae'na califor'nica 40
N. jones'ii 41
N. newber'ryi 41
N. par'ryi 41
Oak Fern 57
Ophioglos'sum califor'nicum 42
O. vulga'tum 42
Parsley Fern 21
Pellae'a andromedaefo'lia 44
P. brachyp'tera 45
P. brew'eri 43
P. brid'gesii 43
P. compac'ta 45
P. mucrona'ta 44
Pepperwort 39
Pillwort, American 48
Pilula'ria america'na 48
Pityrogram'ma triangula'ris 48
Polypo'dium califor'nicum 47
P. glycyrrhi'za 47

P. hesper'ium 46
P. scou'leri 46
Polypody, California 47
Polypody, Western 46
Polys'tichum anderso'nii 52
P. califor'nicum 53
P. dud'leyi 52
P. im'bricans 51
P. lem'monii 53
P. lonchi'tis 50
P. muni'tum 51
P. scopuli'num 53
Pteri'dium aquili'num 49
Running Pine 37
Scouring Rush, Common 29
Scouring Rush, Dwarf 29
Scouring Rush, Northern 29
Scouring Rush, Smooth 29
Selaginel'la asprel'la 56
S. bigelo'vii 54
S. doug'lasii 55
S. han'seni 55
S. orega'na 54
S. scopulo'rum 55
S. walla'cei 56
S. wat'soni 56
Shasta Fern 53
Silverback Fern 48
Spikemoss, Alpine 56

Spikemoss, Blue 56
Spikemoss, Bushy 54
Spikemoss, Douglas' 55
Spikemoss, Festoon 54
Spikemoss, Hansen's 55
Spikemoss, Rocky Mountain 55
Spikemoss, Wallace's 56
Spikemoss, Watson's 56
Spleenwort 15
Sword Fern, Anderson's 52
Sword Fern, California 53
Sword Fern, Common 51
Sword Fern, Dudley's 52
Sword Fern, Rock 51
Sword Fern, Rocky Mountain 53
Thelyp'teris dryop'teris 57
T. phegop'teris 57
Venus-Hair Fern 13
Wood'sia orega'na 58
Woodsia, Oregon 58
Woodsia, Rocky Mountain 58
Wood'sia scopuli'na 58
Water Fern 26
Wood Fern, Coastal 25
Wood Fern, Downy 26
Wood Fern, Sierra 26
Wood Fern, Spiny 25
Wood Fern, Spreading 25
Woodwar'dia fimbria'ta 59

other books like this one, and what they identify:

for eastern North America
- **FLOWER FINDER**—spring wildflowers and flower families
- **TREE FINDER**—all native and introduced trees
- **WINTER TREE FINDER**—leafless winter trees
- **FERN FINDER**—native northeastern and midwestern ferns
- **TRACK FINDER**—tracks and footprints of mammals
- **BERRY FINDER**—native plants with fleshy fruits
- **LIFE ON INTERTIDAL ROCKS**—intertidal plants and animals
- **WINTER WEED FINDER**—dry plant structures in winter
- **BIRD FINDER**—some common birds and how they live

for Pacific coast states
- **PACIFIC COAST TREE FINDER**—native trees, Sitka to San Diego
- **PACIFIC COAST BIRD FINDER**—some common birds, how they live
- **PACIFIC COAST BERRY FINDER**—native plants with fleshy fruits
- **PACIFIC COAST FERN FINDER**—native ferns and fern relatives
- **REDWOOD REGION FLOWER FINDER**—wildflowers and families
- **SIERRA FLOWER FINDER**—wildflowers of the Sierra Nevada
- **PACIFIC INTERTIDAL LIFE**—organisms of pools, rocks and reefs
- **PACIFIC COAST MAMMALS**—mammals, their tracks, other signs
- **PACIFIC COAST FISH**—marine fish, Alaska to Mexico

for Rocky Mt. and desert states
- **DESERT TREE FINDER**—desert trees of CA, AZ, NM
- **ROCKY MOUNTAIN TREE FINDER**—native Rocky Mountain trees
- **ROCKY MOUNTAIN FLOWER FINDER**—wildflowers below tree line
- **MOUNTAIN STATE MAMMALS**—mammals, their tracks, other signs

for a catalog write **NATURE STUDY GUILD**, box 10489, Rochester, N.Y. 14610